THE RAIN AND THE GLASS
99 Poems, New and Selected

Robert Nye

GREENWICH EXCHANGE
LONDON

Greenwich Exchange, London

First published in Great Britain in 2004
All rights reserved

THE RAIN AND THE GLASS
© Robert Nye 2004

Printed and bound by Q3 Digital/Litho, Loughborough
Tel: 01509 213456
Typesetting and layout by Albion Associates, London
Tel: 020 8852 4646
Cover design by December Publications, Belfast
Tel: 028 90286559

Front cover: John Bucklow

Greenwich Exchange Website: www.greenex.co.uk

ISBN 1-871551-41-2

For poems taken from Robert Nye's *Collected Poems* (1995), grateful acknowledgement is made to Carcanet Press who keep that volume in print.

Acknowledgements are also made to the following magazines and periodicals in which some of the new poems first appeared: *Agenda*, *PN Review*, the *Daily Express*, *The London Magazine*, *The Scotsman*, *The Shop: A Magazine of Poetry*, *The Tablet*, and *The Times Literary Supplement*.

The author himself would like to thank both The Royal Literary Fund and The Authors' Foundation for their patronage.

Robert Nye was born in London in 1939. His principal calling is poetry and he has never followed any occupation which interfered with that vocation. He left school at the age of 16, at which time his first poems were published in *The London Magazine*. He lived for six years in a remote cottage in Wales, working on two collections of poems which won him a Gregory Award in 1963. An Arts Council bursary followed the publication of his third book of poems, *Darker Ends* (1969). He has prepared editions of other poets with whose work he feels an affinity: Sir Walter Ralegh, William Barnes, and Laura Riding, and in 1976 he edited *The Faber Book of Sonnets*. A freelance writer since 1961, for many years he supported his independence by contributing book reviews to *The Times* and *The Scotsman*, bringing to the task what the entry about him in the *Larousse Dictionary of Writers* describes as "considerable intelligence and taste, and an infectious love of poetry". In the words of the same source, he is also "an able playwright and a notably uncondescending writer for children, but remains, chiefly, a poet". He has lived since 1977 near Cork, in Ireland. Twice married, he has six children.

Contents

Foreword

Words on the Wind	1
Violin	2
Good-Morning in a Catholic Country	2
The Traveller in the Evening	3
The Cure	4
Opal	6
At Chartreuse de la Verne	7
My Companion	8
The Devil in Me	9
The Clown	10
Touching Treacle	11
About a Maypole	12
The Only Way	13
A Charm against Bad Dreams	14
Dorothy Wordsworth's Sonnet	15
Cockle-Shells at Pagglesham	16
Walking in Cloud	17
Birthright	18
The Rat	19
The Lark at Dayspring	20
Vigils	21
After Simplicius	22
The Spider	23
At the Circus	25
The Task	26
The Well-Spring	28
Pastourelle	29

Winter More	30
An English Education	31
The Devil's Jig	32
A Valediction	33
Finch	34
Song Talk	35
The Cockerel	36
The Prize	37
Down Darkening	39
The Ember	40
O Polly Dear	41
Margaretting	42
Hares Dancing	43
Admonition on a Rainy Afternoon	44
Hospital Incident	45
The Rain in the Eaves	47
The Frogs	48
On a Leaf Used as a Book-Mark	49
Memory	50
The Castle of the Perfect Ones	51
Catching Leaves	52
The Sisters	53
Without Prejudice	54
A Bit of Honesty	55
The Christmas Witness	56
Moon Fever	57
A Charm against Amnesia	58
The Rain Upon the Roof	59
To a Young Poet	60
Childhood Incident	61
Going to the Dogs	63
Riposte	64
Prologue to a Mask of the Seven Deadly Sins	65
In Memoriam John Cowper Powys	66
All Hallows	67
In More's Hotel	68
Reading Robert Southey to my Daughter	69
Interview	71
My Uncle	72

Travelling to my Second Marriage on the
    Day of the First Moonshot   73
Henry James   74
Agnus Dei   75
Fishing   77
Crowson   78
Rough Old Joker   81
A Small Mercy   82
Ropes   83
Not Looking   84
A Trout   85
An Absence of Nettles   86
Gathering Sticks   87
Gone Out   88
Anniversary   89
An Excellent Match   90
A Loaf of Bread   91
The Same Song   92
A Bat in a Box   93
Darker Ends   94
Wideawake Water   95
At Last   96
A Golden Knot   97
The Lark   98
Shadows   99
Familiar Terms   100
Christmas Eve   101
The Stoat   102
Night Watch   103
Dedications   104
Other Times   105
A Moth   106
A Song of Sixpence   107
Listeners   108

Index of titles   109
Index of first lines   113

Tant pis pour le bois qui se trouve violon
Rimbaud

Foreword

One afternoon in 1952 for no apparent reason I fell asleep by a window in the front room of the house in an Essex seaside resort where I was living with my parents. It was winter and rain was beating against the glass. In my sleep, which was deep, I dreamed a poem. In the dream it was night and there was a different house and rain at another window. There was no 'I' in the dream, only this other house and the rain and the glass, and a very strong sense that the dreamer *was* the rain and the glass, and all this coming as words and rhythms heard and felt, blindly, not as things seen. The essence of the dream was perhaps rhythm, but its substance came as words. When I woke I wrote these words down, adding punctuation and (later) a title. I was 13 years old. It seemed to me that for a moment I had fallen awake. It was after this dream that I knew what I had to do for the rest of my life.

This book contains 39 poems written since the publication of my *Collected Poems* in 1995, together with 60 selected from that volume. The order in which the poems are presented is more or less the reverse of chronological, so that the last poem in the book is in fact the earliest, that dream poem.

Most of the poems are as first written, some have been revised over the years in the interests of sound or sense or both, a few (having been revised) are now returned to their original innocent state.

The craft, as has been noted, is long to learn. And the last lesson (like the first) may be that craft at best is only half the story, for poetry is not a product of the will. I have spent my life trying to write poems, but the poems gathered here came mostly when I was not.

Kingsland   Robert Nye
County Cork   Easter 2004

WORDS ON THE WIND

I heard a voice calling:
'Do not be afraid
For blessèd is he
Who is what he was
Before he was made.'

They came on the wind
Those singular words
And on the wind went.
Perhaps all it was
Was the calling of birds?

Perhaps all there is
Is the calling of birds
As they're blown on the wind
And we just mistake it
For singular words?

God knows I don't know
But now night is falling
I am what I was
Before I was made,
And this is my calling.

VIOLIN

Too bad for the wood
If it find itself
A violin—
So Rimbaud said
Who should have known
Being himself
At certain times
A very Strad.

GOOD-MORNING IN A CATHOLIC COUNTRY

'Thanks be to God,' most of the neighbours say
In answer to my casual 'Fine day.'

I like this honour paid by attribute
To someone definite seen at the root
Of everything, whom we can thank together
Even for such a congeries as weather.

THE TRAVELLER IN THE EVENING

The traveller hasteth in the evening
Through a bare landscape like a scooped-out skull.
Clouds scud above his head where he is seeking
To reach a house before the coming storm.
He wears his hat pulled down across his eyes
So we can't read what's written on his brow,
But from the walking-stick dug in to spur
His next stride on, and from the cut-away
Flapped out behind him, we can tell this man
Hastens for pressing reasons of his own.

An evening shade himself, a reveller
Strayed from some love-feast underneath the hill,
He seems a spectre, a sublunary thing.
His trousers if he has them are so tight
It looks at first that he's not wearing any.
His shoes if he is wearing shoes are pumps.
His shadow streams behind him as he goes
And we perhaps are meant to note a hint
Of genitalia, of sex unspent
Between his legs at full stretch in the dusk.

We can't quite see the fury at his back
Which he no doubt has seen, and which now drives
Him headlong down this track, this winter way
Across the fen, though it's a miry slough
Itself, and gulps his feet at every step
So that we might think he will disappear
Before he ever gains his home again.
That's if he has a home. Who knows? Who knows?
All we can say for sure is that this is
A traveller hasting before night. Like us.

THE CURE

'When he was born he cried too much,'
    My mother said, and laughed.
'He grizzled even at my breast,
    I thought he might be daft.

'He whined, he wailed, he caterwauled,
    And if he took a nap
He'd soon wake up to cry again
    As he lay in my lap.

'He had this fever in his blood
    Which made him howl, my dears.
Yet, here's the funny thing, not once
    Did I see any tears.'

She sniffed, and dabbed at her pink nose
    With a lace handkerchief.
The rain upon the window-pane
    Ran down without relief.

'How did you soothe him?' asked my wife,
    'How did you stop his crying?'
My mother smiled, and winked at me
    To show she was not lying.

'I dipped my finger in my gin,'
    She said, 'and let him lick it
Until he was quite satisfied.
    Well, that proved just the ticket!

'I got a good night's sleep at last,'
    She said, 'and so did he.
And after that each time he cried
    I knew the cure, you see.

'I'd found his perfect medicine,
    The thing to keep him quiet.
A suck of Gordon's from my thumb
    Became my baby's diet.'

She nodded then, as one who sees
    Glad days beyond recall.
The rain against the window-pane
    Showed no remorse at all.

'He'd lie there in my arms,' said Mum,
    'Just like a pig in clover,
Laughing his head off all the time,
    My tosspot, half seas over.'

'How long did this go on?' My wife
    Framed the sharp question lightly.
'Oh, no more than a month at most,
    And then not even nightly,

'Only when he refused to sleep
    And kept up that hallooing
Which would have been the death of me
    But for the Mother's Ruin.

'It stopped I'd say when Uncle Ray
    Popped in one day and said
That boy's dead drunk! And so you were!'
    She grinned, and shook her head.

'We had to laugh! You would have laughed!'
    My mother fondly cried.
My wife was trying not to weep
    As she stood by my side,

While as for me I watched the rain
    That wrote my epitaph
And felt like crying, right enough,
    But soon began to laugh.

OPAL

The thing about the opal is
Its fire comes from the imperfections in it.
Different in this regard from other stones—
Not to be prized above them for that reason
But to be valued for a kind of truth
Those others do not have, the truth of showing
The flaw at the root of all, and the beauty of it.

AT CHARTREUSE DE LA VERNE

At Chartrcuse de la Verne the very bees
Were drunk with the coherence of the place.
That monastery stands on holy ground
Once sacred to Diana, where before
Some god without a name was glorified.
Its bees, intoxicated, sing his praises
As surely as they say their paternoster
And hymn Our Lady of the wild green woods,
All in one drone, as wise as it is sweet.
A song of Christ and honey, fire and air!
I heard it once as I stood sober there,
And never since have heard the like elsewhere.

MY COMPANION

Even on good days I can feel him there,
That old familiar stranger at my back
I've never turned round quick enough to catch
A glimpse of, my companion, in pursuit,
Walking when I walk, running when I run,
Keeping his distance from me all this time,
Yet coming nearer lately in some sense
I know about but can't quite comprehend.

I say no more than that I feel at home
Knowing him there behind me, following,
Although he must be tired of the chase
As I am tired of leading him a dance.
One day when he starts limping, I shall limp;
And if he falls down dead that night, what then?
I cannot say I like his company
But what I'll do without it heaven knows.

THE DEVIL IN ME

The devil in me coming to a head
You thought it high time he was taught a lesson
So beat the villain till he fell down dead
Although he had committed no transgression.
Alas within the hour he rose again,
Swollen with indignation, twice as bad,
And would not sink beneath the counterpane
Until you gave him everything you had.
Which done, he let us be a sweet while longer
Before he stirred a final time from sleep
And stood up proud, and angrier, and stronger,
With a malevolence that made me weep.
    He made you weep as well, my dear, as well
    As any woman wept when loved like hell.

THE CLOWN

I saw a man nailed to a tree,
His red blood running down.
A scroll proclaimed he was a king
But he looked like a clown.

His face was white, with parched black lips
Agape as if to grin.
His hands and feet twitched on the tree
Where nails had gone right in.

He had a crown upon his head
But it was made of thorn,
And he was naked as he'd been
The day that he was born.

The blood ran down from that poor clown
And made the green tree red.
My God, he cried, eyes open wide,
I'm only broken bread.

I'm only broken bread, he said,
And red wine running down.
And so beside himself he died,
My king who was a clown.

TOUCHING TREACLE

Treacle, when touched, will always disappoint
The fingers, because stickier than it looks,
Yet still we long to touch it if we can,
To stroke it even, though we know our hands
Cannot caress what draws them to its gleam.
If we could touch what makes us want to touch it
We might become that thing we cannot touch
But treacle would not be more tangible.

ABOUT A MAYPOLE

At Dormans Land I saw a skein of girls
Dancing about a maypole in the sun
With ribbons in their fingers, damoiselles
Weaving the wand in the middle red and white
As they wound round about it, pretty ghosts
In sky-blue dresses for that rite of Spring.

Forever after now when it is Spring
My blood goes dancing with those little ghosts
About a maypole, woven red and white.
At Dormans Land I see you, damoiselles,
In sky-blue dresses, dancing in the sun.
Dance, dance, until the maypole's done, my girls.

THE ONLY WAY
(To Selma Hards)

She tells me when she was a girl and used to point her toe
In dances on the village green on May Days long ago
She always started off too soon, then found to her dismay
The others laughing at her as they went the other way.

'I always went the wrong way round the maypole as a kid.
O why,' she says, 'did I not wait to see what others did?'
Lady, a poet married you because you danced there so.
Your own way round the maypole is the only way to go.

A CHARM AGAINST BAD DREAMS

Sheets washed in rain-water
Then hung out to dry on the west wind
Make good ground for dreaming.

Shoes brushed before night-fall
And set beside the bed heels-under
Will ride away nightmare.

Sleep may then enchant you
And hold you in her arms and grant you
A night without waking.

DOROTHY WORDSWORTH'S SONNET

William was on his way to say good-bye
To his French mistress and their natural child.
The weather, I remember, was quite mild,
Though a bright sun shone fiercely in the sky.
My brother sat, as usual, silently,
Wrapt in his cloak a-top the Dover coach,
Annette upon his mind. I dared not broach
That subject, so I spoke of purity—
Directing his attention to the way
The morning light redeemed the dirty city
Seen from Westminster Bridge. (I could not say
How much I loved him, which was no great pity.)
'Tomorrow will improve on yesterday,'
I told him. 'Look, the prospect's almost pretty!'

COCKLE-SHELLS AT PAGGLESHAM

The smell of cockle-shells at Pagglesham:
That's where I come from, that's where I belong.
Not in the place, not in the place's name,
Though these mean much to me, but in that smell
Of empty cockle-shells cascaded down
Beside a creek, a most particular smell.
Even the first time I encountered it
It seemed a memory of something else.

No doubt some old Sargasso of the heart
Gives me this fact which is unlike all others.
I know my eyes sting at the recollection
And the hairs prickle in the nape of my neck.
I don't know why the unforgotten smell
Of cockle-shells at Pagglesham does this,
Nor why when larger passions cease to move me
So small a thing can bring so much regret.

My mother said she never liked the sea
Because there was too much of it. But shells
Gutted of cockles are a different matter
And their perfume at one remove again.
As for the memory of this deathy smell—
Why it is sweet to me I can't quite say
But sweet it is, sweeter than cockle-shells
At Pagglesham, a breath of Paradise.

WALKING IN CLOUD

Walking in cloud a man becomes
Half cloud himself, and half despair
That he must wear a shroud of air.

BIRTHRIGHT

My mother's mother was a witch
Who cast a natural spell
On a priest's son, my grandfather,
To make him love her well.

She bound him in her long black hair
The night that they were wed
And kept him captive by her craft—
Or so my mother said.

Better believe it. Who am I
For whom no home sufficed,
My mother's birthright to deny,
Half Hecate and half Christ?

THE RAT

I saw a dead rat on the road
And walked straight by, but not before
Half-noting how the creature lay
Snout-upwards in his own bright gore
With claws outstretched to keep or catch
A grip on this too shining day
In which at last he'd met his match.
He had not tried to run away
But turned to fight the fatal thing.
He lay there, robed in blood, a king.
I could not like a rat alive
But that rat's death so fitted him
I stood a moment by the way
And wept because I pitied him.

THE LARK AT DAYSPRING

Up I got and walking early
In the stubble of the barley,
Frost a blessing on the ground,
Heard a lark sing incompletely
In the half-light, then more sweetly
With a small and silver sound.

As the sun rose that true singing
Swelled to greet it, pulsing, ringing,
The lark soaring in the air,
Where he throbbed in perfect glory
Pouring out his morning story
Like a long adoring prayer.

Now that night is over, nearly,
You must tell the truth more clearly.
It is not too late to start.
Like the lark at dayspring turning
To the sun and burning, burning
Sing the song of your whole heart.

VIGILS

Bees (some believe) on Christmas Eve
    Wake from their winter sleep
To hum a honey song of praise
    And night-long vigil keep.

Only the pure of heart they say
    Hear bees or angels sing
These Christmas hymns. I listened once
    And never heard a thing.

Still, I don't disbelieve. Who knows
    What songs the wise heart hears
If it is pure, or not impure,
    And kept awake by tears?

AFTER SIMPLICIUS

Time is a dream and all we do
Will be the same again.
I'll sit like this and talk with you,
Between my hands this cane,
And we shall kiss again, like this,
Again, and then again.

Again, and then again, like this
We'll sit, I'll have this cane
Between my hands, and we shall kiss
And talk, like this, again.
Dear, what I tell you now is true:
Time is a dream and all we do
Will be the same again.

THE SPIDER

Few know as well as I do
   The way the spider spins
Her web of thought and feeling
   Just where the night begins.

She draws out from her entrails
   Each nervous silver line
And weaves them in a pattern
   As fierce as it is fine.

That web extends in circles
   But from each rounded part
A radiating line runs
   Back to the hollow heart.

A final thread's flung upwards
   To where the spider waits
Apart from her creation.
   She squats and masturbates.

It only takes a shiver
   Across the silken mesh
To call the spider downwards
   In quest of other flesh.

She travels down her trap-line
   And feels each separate string
Then follows the vibration
   Out to the tangled thing.

Do not believe those wise men
   Who call the spider cruel.
She's neither cruel nor kindly,
   Nor is the fly a fool.

This web is just a shrouding
   In sense of purest thought.
It is her mind that kills us
   When once we have been caught.

It is pure mind that kills us
   And eats us up, my friends,
Once we have loved the spider
   Where all our daylight ends.

AT THE CIRCUS

LORD GEORGE SANGER'S CIRCUS (*For One Night Only*) WITH HIS FAMOUS ELEPHANTS.
All one wet day we waited for it,
Entering at darkfall the big top
Pitched in a muddy field on the edge of town.

Drumming of rain on that canvas roof!
Lights!
      Music!
            Clowns with sad white faces!
Jugglers and acrobats!
        Fire!
           Horses!
And lo, George Sanger's famous elephants
Trumpeting in behind their stink,
Their trunks erect, their feet so delicate
You might have thought that they were dancing ...

But here's the wonder:
        My little son
Who'd talked of nothing else but elephants
(Because he'd never seen an elephant)
Shut his bright eyes to breathe in elephant
And fell asleep with surfeit of delight
And did not wake until the show was over.

THE TASK

When I was a boy I was set a certain task:
To run and catch falling leaves from a singular tree
That grew in the garden of a great white house
Where a woman lived who was said to be a witch.

Perhaps she was. I never once saw her face
Though sometimes I saw her shadow against the blinds.
I wrote on the leaves her name that I did not know
With my finger dipped in the dark for ink.

So busy was I at my task of catching those leaves
And running about the tree that was one side burning
And the other side green that I never had time to think
Or wonder what I was doing and why I was doing it.

Tonight once more I find myself in the garden
Performing again the ancient impossible task.
Now it's the tree that holds my concentration:
How can one half be green and the other half burning?

As always I'm not watched from the rosy window.
No ring raps cousinly against the glass
To scold me or confer a wordless blessing.
The oldness of my task weighs heavy on me.

But still I write her name on the leaves I catch
Although if you asked me I couldn't say what it is.
I know in the moment of writing I spell her name
And just to do that I must run and catch what I can.

Just to do that I must keep on catching the leaves
By running about the tree that is one side burning
And the other side green. This is my own true task
Set me when I was a boy by the lady of the house.

This is my green and burning one true task
Until the day I die: To run and catch
As many leaves as I can from that singular tree
And to write on the leaves a name I may never know.

THE WELL-SPRING

Happens this spring won't freeze, and that is something.
Must start deep down there underneath the rock
From some substratum where the spirit flows
Bloody and hot, but comes out cold and good
In this place I've scooped clean and filled with pebbles.

I like this well-spring. I pick out such leaves
As might drift in when I'm not here to see
The water has its way, up from the black
Where it begins to where it clearly ends,
Much of it in my mouth to feed my bones.

I have to have a certain quiet degree
Of crystal in me every day to keep
My bones good and be sure I know I walk
With earth between me and the rock, this earth
I cannot get through but the water does.

Water gets through it, and the crystal rests
In me, and is my strength, and makes my bones
Walking the earth. Now when I kneel and drink
There is a skin of ice upon the spring.
I bite this ice and break it with my teeth.

It tastes of spirit and the rock, not earth.
There is no taint of earth or death in it.
I like the ice the more for knowing that
This spring will never freeze or petrify,
Will never freeze right through no matter what.

I eat the bits of ice. I drink the water.
Each is so cold it warms me. I give back
The quick heat lost in coming through the earth.
We are like kinds, this well-spring and myself,
And what we are will never freeze, that's all.

PASTOURELLE

You hear her voice in the long grass:
It whispers Egypt, Egypt as you pass.
You hear it in the wind and rain
Calling one name again, again, again.

You see her eyes in the bright stream:
They stare at you as if you are her dream.
Dazzled with tears of purest light
They wait for night no doubt, and more than night.

Comb the ferns through with your fingers,
Licking the smear of green which lingers.
Here's the purple of herb Robert:
It smells as bad as a dead man's pocket.

Stand still and use that other sense
Which has no tincture of intelligence
To let the woods take root in you
And bring forth leaves in all you say and do.

WINTER MORE

When it was Winter what I saw
Was not enough for my heart's claw.

I wanted the North Wind to blow
Like God the Father shouting No.

My heart was greedy for pure cold;
I wanted icicles of gold.

I wanted Taj Mahals of ice
And no mere Arctic could suffice.

Winter extreme, Winter complete
Was what I longed for in my heat

To reach an absolute North Pole
And know in body and in soul

Some more-than-polar vertigo,
The truth of snow on snow on snow.

This was my secret lust and lore:
I always wanted Winter more.

AN ENGLISH EDUCATION

Before I went to school my grandmother
Taught me to read by reading verse to me.
She'd sit me on her knee and have me point
To words in the big book of nursery rhymes
Which she then chanted like a magic spell.
I learned not just the words but what words do
When they are set to sing and dance together
In unison, the sound and sense as one.

At school I had a teacher called Miss Joyce
Whose joy was choral speaking. She beat time
With a white wand while we declaimed the Psalms.
From her I learned that one deep breath indrawn
Suffices for the saying of a line
With five beats in it, or ten syllables.
But most she taught me how the heart speaks best
When it is given words of praise to say.

My last instructress in the craft of verse
Was a wise woman who'd stopped writing it,
Convinced it could not be the tongue of truth.
She lessoned me in that impossible
Which I now practise all imperfectly—
Still learning how to read from poetry,
Still speaking from the heart in poetry,
Because alas I cannot stop myself.

THE DEVIL'S JIG

The devil's asleep in the place of the dead
And snoring as loud as a pig
When Jesus comes in with a tune in his head
Crying, Give us a bit of a jig!
Hey, give us a jig, Scratch, give us a jig,
Fiddle yer fiddle and give us a jig!

The devil jumps up in the grip of a trance
To do what the master said
And wind up his strings so that Jesus can dance
And wake up and harrow the dead.
Ho, wake up the dead, Scratch, wake up the dead,
Scrape on yer cat-gut and wake up the dead!

Our Lord and old Adam, the devil and all
Go dancing their way round and round,
God knows there was never more hell of a ball
Nor a jig with a jollier sound.
Hi, let's have more sound, Scratch, let's have more sound,
Saw with yer horse-hair and let's have more sound!

Two days and two nights to the fiddle's delights
A very fine dance is led,
Till on the third day to the devil's dismay
Christ dances away with the dead.
Ha, dance with the dead, Scratch, dance with the dead,
Fiddle-come-faddle and dance with the dead!

Our Lord Jesus Christ has danced back from the dead
And taught us to care not a fig
For death and its ways for the rest of our days
By stepping in time to the jig.
So keep up yer jig, Scratch, don't stop yer jig,
Fiddle for ever ye devil yer jig!

A VALEDICTION

There is no more to be said:
Soon enough you will be dead;
Soon enough an end of light
And then everlasting night.

There is no more to be done:
Nothing new beneath the sun;
Not a thing that you can do
That will make more sense of you.

Cry then, cry beyond belief
Like that poor repentant thief
As he died at Calvary:
Jesus, Lord, remember me!

FINCH

The finch, an inch or two of fire,
A feathered green Orfeo,
He bobs and throbs on the barb wire,
Singing in sleet in May, O!
He sings of all and everything
To do with his desire for Spring;
He sings because he has to sing:
In jubilate Deo.

SONG TALK

Some say the nightingale improves his song
By adding new notes to it, year by year,
Correcting any bits he first gets wrong
Until the whole is simple and sincere.

But others say that bird sings from the heart
And does not need to add or change a thing
Because he is inspired from the start
To know what song a nightingale should sing.

I say it does not matter which is right
So long as the bird truly tells his tale;
Nor do you need to understand the night
To sing your heart out like a nightingale.

THE COCKEREL

The cockerel wakes his neighbours up
With rude red shouts.
He sings in scat
A rat-tat-tat
Magnificat.
He has no doubts.

Perched on a dunghill belting out
His hymn of praise,
He magnifies
And glorifies
The morning skies.
I like his ways.

Old cock, old crony, sing for me
Who cannot crow.
O chant it clear
So all can hear
Both far and near:
Co co rico
And *cock-a-doodle-doodle-do.*
Would I could pray as well as you!

THE PRIZE

Darklong I walked in the long dark
Down avenues of a great park.
Winter it was, the trees all bare,
A smell of bonfires on the air
Though no fire burned that I could see
And there was no one there but me.

I thought I walked at the night's noon.
The way was black. There was no moon
And nothing stirred in the deep wood,
Or nothing that I understood.
But then I saw the morning star—
Venus that some call Lucifer.

And all at once I heard the horn
Sound for a death. O note forlorn!
I saw that day-star in the east
And knew the nature of the beast
This blast was blown for. 'Heart,' I said,
'You are the prize, and yet not dead.'

Then down upon my knees I fell
And called to Christ who harrowed hell:
'O Lord, have pity on the hare,
And on the sparrow and the stare,
And in your mercy spare them all
Who have no power on you to call!'

No sooner had I spoken than
Deep in the wood a bird began
To sing, and other birds joined in
Until there was a joyful din
Of little voices, every one
Singing to greet the rising sun.

It rose with all the seraphim
And danced above the park's walled rim,
And those long ways that had been dark
Rang with the linnet and the lark.
Then from that place of darkest night
I went my way in Easter light.

DOWN DARKENING

Down darkening or darkening down—
To not know what it means
To go down darkening or darkening down;
To rest content in mystery
Yet still to seek
The root of meaning,
Its broomstick shadow even,
In this down darkening or darkening down.

What if there is no bright original?
What if down darkening or darkening down
Is all there is to have by way of knowledge?
Go down then darker far than darkening down
To the first broomstick, and beyond the witch.
What's here? What's left at last but down and down
And nothing nothing nothing in the dark?
Better to go on without hope than come
To such conclusion.
Better to rest content in darkening down
Or discontented with down darkening.

THE EMBER

Have you forgotten sitting on the stairs
To read your book?
The taste of sherbet sucked through liquorice?
The slanty look
Of shadows dancing on a deckled page?
These were the simple joys of your young age.

The stairs are ruined and your book long since
Lost power to please,
Now worse than sherbet or sweet Spanish Wood
Has brought you ease.
You can remember but no longer see
Those shadows dancing in their ecstasy.

The fire is almost out, yet where its heart
Once was all flame
A single ember keeps you company.
Call on her name
Who is your Memory, that you may know
Once more the lost delights of long ago.

O POLLY DEAR

Oh how I wish that I was there
With my dear Polly at the fair!
O Polly dear
Why aren't you here?
We were so happy at the fair!

About my feet the grass grows green—
Greener grass I've never seen!
O Polly dear
Why aren't you here?
How happy we were at the fair!

Above my head the night is black—
O my lost love, come back! come back!
O Polly dear
Why aren't you here?
How happy we were at the fair!

Oh how I wish that I was there
With my dear Polly at the fair!
O Polly dear
Why aren't you here?
We were so happy at the fair!

MARGARETTING

As a boy I dreamt of a place called Margaretting.
In my mind it was a village of seven streets,
With a lake perhaps, some swans, and a white church
Where bells rang not just on Sundays, and a grocer's
Selling ginger beer and custard tarts with nutmeg.

I had seen the name on a map of darkest Essex
And the sound of it pleased me as much as Thundersley Glen.
Margaretting: the present participle maybe
Of the verb to margaret, meaning to behave
Or be like the girl who sat next to me in class.

I considered her the quintessence of all things fair
As well as wise and true. Where we made pictures
She had her men lean in the wind when walking
While my men walked upright and looked like art.
I knew then that the Devil was a woman.

And so I came to dream of Margaretting
Where I have never been but always might be.
It is all times and places that I wait for.
It is a scent, a hint, a ghost, a gesture.
It is not heaven or hell but very earth.

One day I'll go there, one day I will get
To the white chapel and ring all the bells
And eat the tarts and drink the ginger beer
And see the swans rise from their ruffled lake
And marry Margaret in Margaretting.

HARES DANCING

Once, once I stood
By a green wood
And watched hares in the snow.
Against the light
They reared upright
As they danced there to and fro.
And the sun stood still
On a silver hill
And the wind forgot to blow.

Those hares ran wild.
I was a child
And tears ran down my face
To see them dance
As in a trance
In that white and holy place.
And the dark night fell
But I knew quite well
I was in a state of grace.

Long, long ago
It was, I know,
And I have other cares.
I lie and weep
And cannot sleep
As pain at my heart's core tears.
I will close my eyes
And see no more lies
But dance with the dancing hares.

ADMONITION ON A RAINY AFTERNOON

Do not suppose your tender touch
Will make her love or even like you much.
There is no Lydian measure in your clutch.

To hold on now were less than sense.
Worse, it might match the long day's decadence.
Wet weather makes the fiddle-strings more tense.

Forego the rain, let go before
All is unstrung, or she may loathe you more
Than you deserve who'd make of her a whore.

Let go, let go, my heart, and take
Your pleasure elsewhere, for Erato's sake,
Whether it's love or music that you make.

HOSPITAL INCIDENT

The boy lies dying in the hospital
And his mother has brought him oranges:
They glow in the green glass bowl by his bed.
All afternoon he considers their shining skins
While the old men in the ward attempt to cheer him:
'Eat up your oranges, cocker, there's a good lad.'

The men's ward and the women's lie side by side.
On summer nights the women sit up in their beds
Brushing their hair, and calling across to the men.
Those oranges burn in the bowl on the boy's locker.
He is sixteen years old. He will never be older.
He stares at that ripe fruit which he will not eat.

Night comes. The lights are lit in both the wards.
The summer air is quick with the noise of insects.
The women call to the men across the grass.
The boy jerks to his feet. He asks the ward orderly
To tie the tape tight which holds his pyjama trousers.
The orderly ties it, and tries to return him to bed.

The boy picks an orange and holds it out, grinning.
'Just once,' he says quietly. 'Like Fred Trueman.'
He is polishing the orange against his groin.
His eyes are bright with tears and angry longing
For what he will never do or know or have.
The orderly shrugs and smiles. He turns his back.

The boy takes three deep breaths of oxygen
Then lurches towards the door on the verandah—
His arm swings over and he bowls full-toss
Into the dark. 'Ladies!' he shouts. 'How's that?'
The orange shatters the square of light opposite,
Smashing the great main window of the women's ward.

The old men don't like this. They ring their bells.
Nurses come running. In the women's ward
They ring their bells too, and call out for their nurses.
The boy does not need nurses, nor these bells.
He lies face down in his blood. He is soon dead.
How's that, ladies? Just once. Pardon him.

THE RAIN IN THE EAVES

The eaves drip rain. It is the eaves
I listen to now as I sit and write.
Some nights the moon comes up in glory
And I scent civet on my sleeves
Where her dress brushed me. But tonight
Just the rain in the eaves tells her story.

It is the saddest tale to tell
And the rain knows that, and tells it well,
Chapter by chapter, bit by bit,
Devil by devil, all of it
In the same drumming monotone—
A voice I could almost believe was my own.

But it is not my tale I write
As I sit up and listen half the night
To the rain in the eaves that mourns and grieves
And frets away at the rotting leaves
Which make it sound like the voice of the dead
Telling her story in my head.

If I could tell her tale I would
But for all I can tell it would do no good.
I tell you the sound of the rain in the eaves
Telling a story no one believes,
Telling a story without any art
I tell you the sound of the rain in my heart.

The eaves drip rain. It is the eaves
I listen to now as I sit and write.
Tomorrow the moon may rise in glory
And there might be civet on my sleeves
Where her dress touched me. But tonight
Let the rain in the eaves tell her story.

THE FROGS

I saw two frogs under a stone
Doing what we do when we are alone.

Belly to back in their foul pool
They did what we do darkly as a rule.

The male frog was a bunch-backed chap.
He clasped his froggy consort to his lap.

The female frog was small and plump.
She shook with lust and took him up her rump.

Their eyes were bright, their mouths agape;
It was a sweet unconscionable rape.

An age I watched them in their slime
Doing what I do now in my black rhyme.

Their frogging done, they had a piss.
Christ send me, quick, another night like this.

ON A LEAF USED AS A BOOK-MARK

A leaf, blown back towards the pool
Against the stream's unwavering flow,
Obeys the wind's soft-spoken wish
To have it so.

So once was I instruction's fool
Upon the surface of delight,
Compelled to contrariety
By day, by night.

You took me in your thrifty hand,
You plucked me from the burning brook;
You dried me out and cured me
In your good book.

Now no more flotsam, I'm the mark
Which tells you how much you have read.
I who was wind-blown and alive
Lie here, not dead.

MEMORY

The Lady Memory disguised in moonlight
Walks the walled garden that I call my mind.
She is the mother of the other Muses;
If you approach her gently you may find
Her shadow is a nightingale, her dress
Some silken thought of long-spun tenderness.

Memory's face reminds me of her daughters
Who once were the delight of my despair.
I have forgotten much, but still remember
The way they sang their songs and combed their hair
On a green hillside where a grove of trees
Made music like a swarm of summer bees.

Peace to those beauties who have left me here
With my own words to eat, a bitter diet
Sweetened by drinking from the Pierian spring.
Good morning, Memory; it is your quiet
I must learn now, not so much reticence
As knowing little can improve on silence.

THE CASTLE OF THE PERFECT ONES

You'll eat no honey in that bee-hive house
(They need no sweets who are themselves so pure)
But in your ears a buzz of holy hymns
Will sound all day, all night, immaculate,
Making the door vibrate on its cracked hinges.
What would you give to pass that door again
And see the stars from the shelving side of the hill!

The prick of perfection lengthens any note
By one exacting half ... So will they stretch you,
Those moral musicians, to your highest pitch
And half a time beyond it. You will know
You are in royal purgatory all right,
A voice in the eternal choir that sings
From the dark tower at the back of the north wind.

Whether this is your home is not the question.
Once in the Castle of the Perfect Ones
Better to be a perfect one yourself
Than to go mad longing for imperfections.
It could be worse. At least you will be faultless
And have no need of honey, stars, or sex:
O pure O self-complete O perfect fool.

CATCHING LEAVES

The boy you were caught leaves that fell
From trees he could not name.
The man you are must try to tell
Rowan from ash, yet run as well
To catch each falling flame
And hope upon its fame.

THE SISTERS

Quick snow is falling, melting as it falls;
She stands between the fireplace and the night
Watching each soft flake flower on the pane,
Half-listening to her sister playing scales—
Their old piano's keys that click and stick—
While in the grate coals crackle together.

These things are more real to you than the scene
You know on waking, but are not a dream:
Notes rising, falling, tired music talking
About the instrument on which it plays;
A firelit room, uncurtained; two sisters
Themselves more slow to vanish than the snow.

Oh, who are they? And where is this grey house?
You have seen one sister perhaps, though not
At a winter window all mothed over.
The details of the vision fall apart;
It was your need first drew them together
Into a storm of changes and desire.

Still, do not doubt that soon enough you'll stand
Between night and the sisters, in the porch
Of the old house, hearing that piano.
And when the music stops and the door opens
Who will you say you are, and why come hither
Out of a world where snow melts as it falls?

WITHOUT PREJUDICE

To Spindle, Shears, and Rod,
Solicitors for God:
Dear madams, ref. the part
Enclosed herewith, my heart—
Please note this doesn't fit
The rest of the love kit
Supplied me by our father,
Your client, being rather
Too big to go with my head
Yet not big enough in bed.

A BIT OF HONESTY

Love is the name they give out in Tasmania
To Traveller's Joy, which some call Virgin's Bower.
The thing itself is sweet, though not as mania
Would have us say, nor bitter in its flower
As those made mad by it sometimes protest.
It is as good a plant as all the rest—
No less, no more. In English parts, you see,
The name for this same thing is Honesty.
Here's honesty for you. Long may it live!
I'd give you love, if I had love to give.

THE CHRISTMAS WITNESS

I call midwinter back to hear you cry
O look at that, my dear! seeing some twig
By the frost's kiss or a soft touch of snow
Abruptly gifted with how bent a grace.
You were the Christmas witness all December
Once it came down to broken sticks and stalks
Surprised into a glory of themselves,
Making me heed and keep that festival
In which dead things achieve a kind of life
Just because frozen vapour blesses them.
Without such lessons in the art of solstice
I would see nothing much worth keeping here.

MOON FEVER

This is the scene to which I keep returning:
The moon is in her shroud, the sky is burning,
Under the streaming stars a heron stands
Like a sickle dipped in feathers; on the sands,
Beside where she is fishing, a silver eel
And speckled trout lie spread in a broken wheel.

I see the heron shiver from her trance
And rise upon the gleaming air askance.
I burn for her, yearning to follow after...
But am brought down to earth by your wise laughter
Who call this my moon fever, kissing me
On my hot eyes to stop the things I see.

A CHARM AGAINST AMNESIA

No name you know reminds you now
Of who you are or why you go
Alone about your trouble in the snow.

Forgetting whom you would forget
You have forgotten more than that
And lost your mind's distinctive alphabet.

So if you trace your footprints back
To where you started, will that track
Supply the sure identity you lack?

The character of snow is white.
You cannot find your own delight
From marks made on it by your appetite.

Do not despair. There is one name
Which being known will make it plain
That you and wasted snow are not the same.

Call up the faces you recall
And see if from among them all
One hurts your heart and makes even cold tears fall.

That half-loved other is your fate—
Her name can turn you from hell's gate
And bring you home again before too late.

THE RAIN UPON THE ROOF

Listen. It is the rain upon the roof
Telling of who you loved but not enough,
Whispering of what is otherwise elsewhere.

It would be sweet on such a night to die,
Kissing another's lips, touching darkly,
Hearing the soft rain falling everywhere.

Save that the rain has voices which complain
You never loved enough, you were unkind,
You ran away, you left your heart nowhere.

Come back! Come back! The rain's regret may cease
But I will love you till my dying breath
And after, if there's after anywhere.

TO A YOUNG POET

In a muck sweat you quarrel with them all—
The knights of the Round Table, squab and tall,
Sat down to meat.

There is a glamour on the hall: plates come
And go just as the diners wish, though some
Refuse to eat.

They say you have come here to spoil their feast
Whose real offence is innocence. At least
You took no seat.

See now the chessmen playing, square to square,
This game that has no purpose but despair
Or twin defeat.

You are a pawn in Camelot's strange chess,
Fit only to be sacrificed, or less,
Your play complete.

Let them say this of you when you are dead:
Although he lost his heart he kept his head
And did not cheat.

CHILDHOOD INCIDENT

One summer day at noon in our family kitchen
In my twelfth year I watched my mother cooking
The Collected Poems of Elizabeth Barrett Browning.

This was, I must admit it, a dirty book.
I had picked it out from an even dirtier junk-stall
Down in the market, near the church that used the incense.

Mrs Browning, as I remember, cost me sixpence—
Which was all my pocket money for a week—
But I forked out for her gladly on account of her famous love.

Alas as I took the book from the Pakistani stall-keeper,
Wiping the dirt of the years from it with my shirt sleeve,
This funeral came out of the church that used the incense...

Back home, my mother saw red at the sight of Mrs Browning
And when, in my stammering, I blurted out about the Pakistani
And then the purple coffin—well, it was just too much!

My mother took Elizabeth Barrett Browning in a pair of
                              fire-tongs
And deposited her in the oven, turning the gas up high,
Remarking that this was the way to kill all known germs.

I feared then that what I would see would be the burning
Of Elizabeth Barrett Browning in our family kitchen;
But, praise to God, my mother knew her regulos.

I remember the venial smell of the baking
Of Elizabeth Barrett Browning in our family kitchen.
I can still see those pages that curled and cracked,

And the limp green leather cover that peeled away like lichen
From the body of the book, and the edges turning gold,
And the hot glue's hiss and bubble down the spine.

But most clearly I recall as if this was just yesterday
An odd but quite distinct and—yes—*poetic* scent
Which arose from the remains of Mrs Browning's Poems

When they came out baked and browned from my mother's
oven
And lay steaming there on the table in the family kitchen.
It was, I swear to God, a whiff of incense.

GOING TO THE DOGS

Come Friday night my father's public vice
Was a greyhound track. He took me there twice.
Most of his life his own sad way he went,
So going to the dogs with me was different.

The electric hare, the eager racing hounds,
Tick-tacks in their white gloves, fistfuls of pounds—
The magic of that place and its event!
Oh, to me going to the dogs was different.

To choose a trap my poor Dad bruised his wits
Perusing form, and when that failed had fits
Of asking me my fancies. What this meant
For us made going to the dogs quite different.

Once the choice dog in the pre-race parade
Excreted what looked like bad marmalade.
'A sign,' my father said, 'from heaven sent!
You do know going to the dogs is different?'

He'd urge his favourite home with passionate cries.
The keenest still brings tears into my eyes:
'Come on, my son!' It was an accident
Which our dear going to the dogs made different.

I can't remember what my old man won;
God knows he lost much more in the long run.
His coat was shabby and his hat was bent,
But going to the dogs I found him different.

I do recall my father shook my hand
When our dog came in first. Now understand:
Some of us gamble when our hearts are spent.
My going to the dogs is not so different.

RIPOSTE

Above all other nights that night be blessed
On which my grandam rose from her sweet rest
Woke by a nightingale whose passionate song
Rang in the moonlight, Keatsian and long.
My grandmother threw open wide her door
And listened for a minute, not much more;
Then, when sufficient nightingale she'd heard,
Cried out: *Right! Just you bugger off, you bird!*

PROLOGUE TO A MASK
OF THE SEVEN DEADLY SINS

I am said to be made in the image of a mystery
Which may never be effaced however marred.
The likeness of God lies in the correspondence of the will.
Adam ate of the tree of the knowledge of good and evil.

It is not known whether that fruit was sweet or bitter,
Nor if without it the mind would have had a better taste.
You may suppose your own death to be a mistake
At least until you have been mistaken by it.

Meanwhile we will have sin to be going on with—
Which consists of so many little sips of the grave,
Original and actual: the sin of birth
And the seven sins of contradiction to eternal grace.

Glory be to the Father and to the Son and to the Holy Ghost.
We can't change human nature but God may
By means of a specific antidote
Which is called Christ and tastes like bread and wine.

IN MEMORIAM
JOHN COWPER POWYS
1872—1963

Knowing the horror of the house
More intimately than its mere ghosts,
You practised to unstitch
The mirror from its silver
And write down your name without wondering who.
O Prospero, no elegy for you.
You have been sent to Naples, that is all,
And this bare island is the barer for it.

ALL HALLOWS

Once as a child I saw the willows
Across the river at All Hallows,
Each one distinct although six miles away.
What brought them close and brings them now again
Sharp to the mind's eye like an icon of it?
An orthodox theology of tears.

IN MORE'S HOTEL
(for Aileen)

Wasn't it just that
We touched for the first time
The mother string
The pearls are threaded on?

Or was it especially
A key, a Bible—
A litany of chance
Which found again
Would spell us close
As we were then
In More's hotel,
Learning our alphabet?

Last night it was cloud
Against the pane, twice
You dreamt it.
This morning I turn on a tap and water
Is water alone, relating
To keys and Bibles
By a cordial difference,
Not very likely, but all the same
Married and holding together well.

READING ROBERT SOUTHEY
TO MY DAUGHTER

Mr Robert Southey had the makings of a haberdasher
With a candy-striped shop in Bristol or Bath,
A secondhand carriage and a bow-legged mistress
With Jacobin leanings; but ambition and his aunt
Drove him to verse—
For which grand vice
He had no gift, only
A self-consuming facility.

Mr Robert Southey had the honour
Of wearing the Coleridges as his albatross.
Bad Lord Byron made his name rhyme with mouthy
And dignified him with fire also
In his Vision of Judgment.

At worst Southey R was a creepy crawly turncoat
Using little epics as tickets of admission
To the lower reaches of what he thought Society.
At best this esquire was a man who was better
Than anything he wrote. Coleridge said
His library was his wife.

O sweet O prolific O mediocre R
O ramblingly gallant and unimportant S
I remember how after the penultimate breakdown
Worn out with hacking you trotted up and down
Just stroking the spines
Of your seventeen thousand leather-bound concubines.

Mr Southey, man of letters, you worthy laureate
With such a thirst for righteous justice,
You once saw Shelley plain

And didn't care for it.
'What a dreadful thought of his wife's fate,'
You said, Sir, 'what a dreadful thought
Must have come upon him when he saw himself
About to perish by water!'
Mahomet was no better.

O Robert O Southey if poor Percy Shelley
Screamed like a peacock, you clucked like a hen.
You had a kind heart but you geared it to royalties
And pensioned it off when the best time came.
Yet tonight, Robert Southey, I thank you by name
For the measure of a story you took and made better:
Not too fast, not too slow, not too hot, not too cold,
Not too hard, not too soft, not too long, not too short,
But just right for my Goldilocks—
Too young to say thank you
Herself, but who loves you
For loving just-rightness;
Bob of the Bears,
Our Southey friend.

INTERVIEW

What's it like, though, being you?
The old dog growls and bristles. This is his favourite question.
Answers win prizes. Nothing interests him more.
Inspired by the pursuit of his own tail
He has written his poems to find out what he smells like,
And now here's another dog, a dog-fancying thoroughbred,
Just down from Oxford, trained to the minute,
On heat and eager to do some of his sniffing
For him, and to declare the crap remarkable.
Woof woof, the old dog says, *bow wow.*
I'll show you where I buried my gift!

MY UNCLE

My uncle's hands were the colour of tobacco.
He sat and he listened to the river rattle.
He dreamt of logic.

My uncle's eyes were the colour of cider.
He sat and he listened to the rain coming on.
He dreamt of Dunkirk.

My uncle's hair was the colour of Bibles.
He sat and he listened to the Tilley lamp's hiss.
He dreamt of luck.

My uncle's face was the colour of allotments.
He sat and he listened to the tick of the clock.
He dreamt of forgiveness.

Now my uncle is dead and his bones are in the ground
And I sit and I listen to the river rattle
And I sit and I listen to the rain coming on
And the Tilley lamp's hiss and the tick of the clock
And my aunt making cakes in the kitchen.

TRAVELLING TO MY SECOND MARRIAGE
ON THE DAY OF THE FIRST MOONSHOT

We got into the carriage. It was hot.
An old woman sat there, her white hair
Stained at the temples as if by smoke.
Beside her the old man, her husband,
Talking of salmon, grayling, sea-trout, pike,
Their ruined waters.

A windscreen wiper on another engine
Flickered like an irritable, a mad eyelid.
The woman's mouth fell open. She complained.
Her husband said: 'I'd like
A one-way ticket to the moon.
Wouldn't mind that.'

'What for?' 'Plant roses.' '*Roses*?' 'Roses,
Yes. I'd be the first rose-grower on the moon.
Mozart, I'd call my rose. That's it.
A name for a new rose: Mozart.
That's what I'd call the first rose on the moon,
If I got there to grow it.'

Ten nine eight seven six five four three two one.
The old woman, remember her, and the old man:
Her black shoes tapping; his gold watch as he counted.
They'd been to a funeral. We were going to a wedding.
When the train started the wheels sang *Figaro*
And there was a smell of roses.

HENRY JAMES

Henry James, top hat in hand, important, boring,
Walks beautifully down the long corridor
Of the drowned house just off Dungeness
At the turn of the century. It is 3 p.m. probably.
It is without doubt October. The sun decants
Burgundy through high windows. The family portraits
Are thirteen versions of the one face, walking
On the thick trembling stalk of Henry James.
It is a face which looks like the face of a goldfish
Fed full of breadcrumbs and philosophy, superbly
Reconciled to its bowl. The difference
Between Henry James and a goldfish, however,
Is that Henry James has nostrils. Those nostrils observe
An exquisite scent of evil from the library.
Henry James goes beautifully on his way. His step
Is complicated. (He nurses an obscure hurt. It is this
Which kept him from active service in the sex war.)
Listen and you will hear the trickle of his digestive juices—
Our author has lunched, as usual, well—
Above the sweetly unpleasant hum of his imagination.
His shoes make no squeak and he deposits no shadow
To simplify the carpet. Henry James
Turns a corner. Henry
James meets Henry
James. Top hat, etcetera. Henry James
Stops. Henry James stares. Henry James
Lifts a moral finger. 'You again!'
He sighs. 'How can you be so obvious?'
Henry James blushes and Henry James flees and Henry
James goes beautifully on his way, top hat
In hand, important, boring, he walks down
The long life-sentence of his own great prose.

AGNUS DEI

On the shore
At the bend of the rock
A shrine:
Three ram skulls on a wall of pebbles.

A wall assembled by human hands,
Not looking natural in this place.
Altars never do.

The skulls all facing out to sea.
To the left, burnt
Into the rock, a capital letter A.
To the right, higher up, looking
Away, another (smaller) skull: a lamb's maybe.
Below, beyond the wall, a hollow
Where black ashes blow,
Stirred by the wind off the sea,
The rain, the grey haar.
To the right, down behind
A bush of thorns
On a narrow ridge
A small rectangular piece of marble,
Wafer-thin, depicting
A ewe with her lambs.

Below, a nail driven into the rock
And the nail holding
A scalp of seaweed,
And the seaweed brown and long
Like the hair of a young girl, a widow.

Above, the low cliff leaning,
The heather growing.
Great knots of roots hanging loose like severed nerves.
The rain grey and the sky falling through the thorns.

All three skulls having seaweed strips laid over them
Like hair, like a young girl's hair,
Like widowing.

FISHING

At thirteen he went fishing for stars.
Either for lack of hooks or love of the strict twine
Which could be taught to shiver in the hand
He fished for them, saying he fished for crabs.

No bait gets glory. He used mussels.
After school he had searched the hard
And taken plenty when the tide was out;
Now each agape, its matter manifest,
His greed made fast with a half-Gordian knot
In a new context, and sent back to the dark
About its tacit business. He felt sure
Some star that lurked or smouldered in the net
Of stars below the surface could be caught.

Crab after crab came up, acknowledging
His wasteful magic and his innocence,
But still no star rose clinging to a shell.
Once, twice, he thought he had one, but
Only an unlucky starfish floundered, half-wound
In the sea-stained twine, mocking star-need.
Sick of ambition, tired of self-deceit,
He lost his sleight of hand, let all his gear
Ride with the tide, and sat and watched the moon.

Later he learned how not to fish too much—
Or, rather, how to fish for more than stars
With less than mussels or a singing line.
He fished for nothing. And he caught the sea.

CROWSON

He died at the proper time, on Christmas Day
As we sat down to dinner—an old man
With no friends and no vices, blindly mean
With the kind of love that goes with being clean,
His chief possessions a sour bar of soap,
A flannel which reeked of him, and a steel comb
He used to keep his dry grey hair in order
Over the face as hard and proud as a doorknob;
A sick old man, but acting out his illness,
A broken man, but whole and straight in cunning,
A man whom no one loved or liked or pitied,
Whom we had wished would die, for the work's sake.
And yet, I think, I did not wish him harm.

Well he was dead at last, on Christmas Day,
And spoiled our dinner. 'Just like him,' said Twitch,
'To go and die now, after seven months
Of not quite dying. Just like him to save
His death for the wrong time, when no one's ready.
Who wants to lay out a corpse on Christmas Day?
It would serve him right if we left him, eh?'
And I agreed (although I was dismayed
Not to feel much beyond an amateur's
Distaste for death), nodding in a paper crown,
Grinning at brother Twitch across a table
Set out with crackers, beer, cheap cigarettes.

Dinner completed and our bellies full,
Half-cut we went to Crowson's room.
He lay, the oxygen mask ridiculously sucked
Into his blue mouth, fish-eyes mocking us.
Beside the neat bed, on the locker,
His watch ticked fussily; his corpse

Scarcely disturbed the counterpane's perfection,
So thin he had become in these last days.
Twitch belched. 'We'd better get him over with.'

And then Twitch bullied
That sticky carcass, punched it here and there
About the bed, about the usual business:
A bag of bones shoved rudely in death's costume.
He mocked the stale flesh, fey in this last gesture—
'A Christmas present, darling'—tying a bow
On the penis, where a knot would have done,
Flirting with the shroud
As if it were the dress of some gay girl,
Taking revenge for all the dead one's age
And ugliness, knowing he would come
To this too soon—and, most of all,
For spoiling our Christmas dinner.

This is no elegy, for I did not love you,
Crowson, old man smelling of soap and tuberculosis;
Surely, for all my wrong, I did not love you
As queer Twitch did, who used you then so cruelly.
And yet, I think, I did not wish you harm.
Am I to blame for what he did to you?
The question in its asking answers 'Yes':
For where did Twitch begin and such fear end
As made me cold, incapable of tears
Or useful rage till this? and in these words
Which cannot warm you now, nor yet avenge
The insult you did not feel in my name,
The bullying no buffet could atone,
Nor prayer nor haunting expiate.

It was my faint white heart which hit you there.
It was my greed of self deflowered you
And bruised you in your death, which you thought perfect.
To ask forgiveness were another insult—
I will ask nothing but that you forget
You ever knew me, as I would forget
The big day I was born, keeping in mind
The day you died. I am forgetting now
In hope I will remember you more clearly
And in your memory wish no harm more dearly.

ROUGH OLD JOKER

He can cut straight down oak, to shape it well,
Just the right point, to make each piece a stake
For a white fence to keep black cattle out;
Yet with each blow he gasps as if the blade
Bit through his bone, and he the rough old joker
Who needed shaping, straightening, made sharp
To drive, or be down-driven, in the earth.
And is there tree-love in the way his hands
Chase down hewn sides, stripping the spills clean off,
Holding the finished stake up to the sun?
Or hate, perhaps, of knowing how this stood
As he has not, long in a growing wood?
In love or out, he knows his work will stand
After he has a longer stake in land.

A SMALL MERCY

Down in the wood the boys walk wild
Hunting for badger and fox;
Afraid of the dark, obeying its curse,
They kill what the dark loves.
Poet, be grateful they do not run
Nor hammer yet at your door,
To drive your pen through your open eye
And follow the night to its source.

ROPES

Watching the old man and the young man
Take ropes from round about the belly
Of the hay-waggon, you said,
'See how the old man coils and curls his rope
And brings it straight to hand,
While the young man leaves his ungathered.'
I knew that you looked down on what I'd wasted
But had not care enough to take it up
And make a neatness of it for your sake.

NOT LOOKING

You notice I never look at you when I speak?
Perhaps you have seen in this something crooked—
A fear of meeting your eyes? You would be right
So to think, for my shame of your knowing is such
I'm frightened of your gaze clean through me
Proving my meaning little to you. Yet it is not just this.

I have a way of not looking, as you see,
Which is also part of a way of seeing.
If I do not return the long stare you offer
To search me with, and you might wish I'd learn,
It is because your presence is too sharp,
Your eyes too dear for my eyes, being poor.

I was never exactly frank, you know.
Besides, it's suitable to talk to smoky air
Knowing you near at hand, inhabiting
The corner of my eye, and half my heart.
If I looked straight at you I might say much;
Might even speak of love, which would not do.

A TROUT

Waiting for you, I sat and watched a trout
And found some warp of comfort in the thought
That I might catch or counterfeit his style
Of silence, to and fro, a subtle fool
In the dark places of the yielding stream,
But in that deeper water where you dream.

Forgive me that I have no gentleness
To be at home with you, nor business
To know you thoroughly, and only you.
With nothing done and nothing much to do
I wait to take you coldly by the hand,
Shaken with love I cannot understand.

AN ABSENCE OF NETTLES

I like nettles, but I took
An old scythe for your sake
To clean the way where you would walk
And make it possible
For your foreshadowed flowers.

An evening I worked there,
And another, longer; gripping
The ancient handles with a clumsy craft,
Swinging the rusty blade about my knees,
Crouched to listen to it.

The keen heads of nettles
Lopped without pity
Were raked and carried up
To a black-hearted bonfire;
The shaven earth was ready.

I plucked out such roots
As the hands can find,
And cast away pebbles;
Weeding and watering
My own grave.

But now—no flowers have come
To fit your shadows;
The earth will not accept
The seeds you sow. And who can care for
An absence of nettles, an ungrowing place?

GATHERING STICKS

Snow in the wind and pine-smoke blown back
Down the awkwardly patched-up chimney-stack
On her house that's at home by the wood.
Gathering sticks in the frosty dell
I stop to watch that smoke I know well
Which has come from the fire of her mood.

Sticks will be chopped and new water drawn
From the spring in the side of a winter dawn
By others, that's understood,
But will they turn back with cleaner hearts
Through snow and wind to where the smoke starts,
And with better fire in their blood?
Perhaps they'll just turn, as I turn now,
Not knowing why, not caring how,
With a love that does no one much good.

GONE OUT

Whenever you leave the house I write a poem—
To answer you or bring your questions home?
When you are here my words belong to you,
You take my breath, not as you used to do,
But for sufficient purposes of speech.
You hang upon my language like a leech.

Yet when you've gone an hour the poem fades
And I have little left but blots and shades
Of meaning, and I mean all that I say,
Which draws me out to stand and watch the way
Through the long valley, hoping you'll come back
To give my words the simple truth they lack.

ANNIVERSARY

This is the wooden wedding—
Five years marred or married.
You came of your strength,
I went of my weakness,
To a time where one said, 'I love you'—
Meaning, 'I am lost. Find me!'—
And the other could not sleep in an empty bed.

Now we sleep too well together
And our separate hearts dream variously.
Such self-caressing dreams...
You have learned my weakness, and it suits you.
I have wasted your strength, and it chokes me.
And yet you speak of this
As an anniversary. And so it is.

We will celebrate our wooden wedding
With poems written by sentimental liars
Who found love easy, a comfortable sun
To shiver under in chill complaisance,
And not as it is—the difficult moon
Crying 'Adore me! Adore me!' and then turning
Her naked back on mortal adoration
To go whoring after other moons, other devourers.

It is an occasion for happiness
And we are happy in our perfect ruin,
Being wooden both and hacking at each other
In the name of truth, though it be only fretwork.
Five years marred or married—
Time enough for regret perhaps
In the next five, in the happier returns,
When the heart has turned to tin.

AN EXCELLENT MATCH

I am your glass, and mirror everywhere
The fires you burn to see, or fear to be;
The man you wish you were, I am for you,
Reflecting who you are in what we do;
Yet I am yours too much, too perfectly—

For look, our likeness has an end, and there
Beyond the glass, deeper than your self-looking,
I rage, in blank suspicion, and half-mocking,
Completed by the knowledge I can share
Those images you give me, your reflections,
Though these shine otherwise, in false directions.

It makes no difference even when the glass
Grows dark with more than night, or streaked with day
Larger than likely. Radiance and stain
Fall on you in a cold familiar way,
Fixed in a constancy I cannot pass.
The colour black is busy here, that's plain.

A LOAF OF BREAD

I went to the road for food, and found
Common surprise in a loaf of bread,
Holding my breath with the breath of it
And knowing that when I breathed again
It would indeed be morning and a loaf of bread
Clean in the carton there with other
Necessary purchases
Of a son unprodigalled, trying to play father.
I had not thought I could be so astonished.

Bread! I sat under the hedge
Out of a hungry wind, and the just-baked loaf
Was matter of fact as I sank my teeth
Into its crust and nibbled, then took
Swift bites out of its good and risen wholeness.
If I'd remembered I'd have sung for joy
Just to myself and the loaf in the commonplace morning—
Joy at dismissing for ever, or the time being,
Guilt at the boy I was for standing
Outside shop windows, sly nose squashed flat
Against the pane, dreaming on galleons and castles
Of cream and pastry, marshmallow, doughnut, shortbread,
Until I thought I'd faint for want of those
Unnecessary sweets which were all I wanted.

I didn't remember till now, and now's too late.
'The birds have been eating the bread again,' you say,
Cutting the bad part out.
                    Thus satisfied—
With bread and the perfect alibi—how could I sing?

THE SAME SONG

You dream a song and I begin to sing it
In a false voice, and so the song is ruined
That was word-perfect in your head. In anger,
You tell me to be silent. 'Still, how strange
That you should sing the same strange song I'm dreaming.
Perhaps I hummed or drummed it? and you heard.'

No, music, I've no natural explanations.
You did not sing—but I have mocked your song
In broken accents, for my own amusement.
One day with a true voice I'd like to tell
How sometimes we catch breath and sing together
The same strange song, knowing we need no other.

A BAT IN A BOX

The long cold cracked and I walked in the cracks
To pay the rent for the first time in weeks
And pick our post up from the farm on the top road.

That done— 'Has your son,' said the farmer's wife,
'Ever seen a bat in a box? I have one
You could take back to show him.'

And I imagined how a bat in a box
Would beat its bloodshot wings, and comb itself
With greedy claws, and eat up flies and beetles;

And how, when hanging by the wing-hooks, it
Would sleep, long ears tucked under, as if cloaked:
And how its tameness might in fact confound me.

I did not take it, back down through the snow
To show my son.
                    Why did I not do so?

To tell you, I would have to undo winter,
Thaw my bare heart and waste its bitterness,
Losing the wry frost with some deeper drifts.

A bat,
        in a box.
                    Just think of it.

DARKER ENDS

Here's my hand turned to shadows on the wall—
Black horse, black talking fox, black crocodile—
Quick fingers beckoning darkness from white flame,
Until my son screams, 'No! chase them away!'

Why do I scare him? Fearful of my love
I'm cruelly comforted by his warm fear,
Seeing the night made perfect on the wall
In my handwriting, if illegible,
Still full of personal beasts, and terrible.

Abjure that art—it is no true delight
To lie and turn the dark to darker ends
Because my heart's dissatisfied and cold.
To tell the truth, when he is safe asleep,
I shut my eyes and let the darkness in.

WIDEAWAKE WATER

Washing sleep away in a bowl of warm rain,
Or with fistfuls of snow, or a melted moon,
Have you never wondered whether your dreams
In the jealous bed are not worth the dreaming?
Whether your whispers to death in the dark
Are less than the gossip of wideawake water?

Others there are who will greet you more gently
And kiss you less softly than wideawake water,
Less honest than water, in love with your dreams.
But I shall not love you for what you imagine,
For more than you dream, or less than you hope,
Washing sleep away in a bowl of warm rain.

AT LAST

Dear, if one day you hear my heart,
Under your cheek, forget to start
Its life-long argument with my head,
Do not rejoice that I am dead
And need some graver sort of bed,
But say: 'At last he's found the art
To hold his tongue and lose his heart.'

A GOLDEN KNOT

In the small hours of the needful night
I watch you comb your rainy hair
And braid it up in a golden knot.

The tortoiseshell in the ember-gleam
Like glazed frost on a silver thaw
Trickles bleak with its own dewiness.

The bed—narrow, cold; a bleb of blood
On the pillow. Your powder pots
And puffs snow-pollen the black mirror.

And is this love: the needless need
To hang myself in a golden knot?
I do not know, but love you needfully.

THE LARK

The lark from his nest in a hoofprint springs
Up, up, up, up, trilling dew from his wings,
And busily rests, and sings, and sings.
I watch and listen, wondering why
His song's sad sweetness, a laughing sigh,
Reminds me only that I must die.

SHADOWS

Seek not to be her shadow for
When night comes shadows go
Into the darkness following
Her footfalls to and fro,
Bewildered by her wandering
In the bewildering snow.

Do you suppose your silences
Will warm her shadowy heart?
Or that by lying at her feet
You'll learn her truthful art?
You might as well adore the moon
Where shadows end, and start.

FAMILIAR TERMS

You say I love you for your lies?
  But that's not true.
I love your absent-hearted eyes—
  And so do you.

You say you love me for my truth?
  But that's a lie.
You love my tongue because it's smooth—
  And so do I.

You say they love who lie this way?
  I don't agree.
They lie in love and waste away—
  And so do we.

CHRISTMAS EVE

On Christmas Eve in ivory air
I drag the old moon by the hair
And trot her through the cobbled snow.

The dark is bright as Calvary.
The naked stars across the black
Web of the night crawl spiderly.

Child, sleep while you can. Tomorrow
I will tell you another story.
Now ride in your dreams the mare Glory,
The stud Death, and the wild colt Sorrow.

THE STOAT

As I walked home a stoat ran round
About me with a womanish sound
Dancing neither high nor low
On an oblique and wily toe,
Eyes like blue cinders in the snow.

Those eyes so used to rat and hare
Fixed mine in a moon-blinded stare
Until I saw you everywhere:
Your dress that drift of smothering snow,
Your face her face, your step her slow
And rampant dancing, in and out,
And up and down and round about,
Until I felt the hot flesh stir
Between my legs, but not for her,
Nor yet for you, and standing still
On whited ground, against my will,
I felt my heart leap to my throat
And cry out for the dancing stoat.

NIGHT WATCH

Watching for my son to fall asleep, I fell asleep first
And woke in a dream to watch him sleep in this world
              (of all probable worlds worst)
Where he must wake in nightmare, not born free,
And nod with one eye open, on me.

Not that I would love him for heaven's sake or, worse,
Make him immortal with a curse.
Dreaming he slept I kept him safe from harm
Who was keeping me awake, and my heart warm.

Lullabies, my jackanapes, are out of date
But to remember them it is not too late:
Sing hushabye then, however much music it take,
However I wake watching for my son to wake.

DEDICATIONS

Begrudged by the promising pencraft of my name—
On the flyleaves of books I thought were mine—
Dedicating each poem to you as if
It hoped its nine letters would be read
Into the classic authorship, and free-hearted
Of Love-until-our-names-are-both-forgotten
(In such shorthands as half-admired their remembrance)
I could not yet refuse to sign myself
Or much regret you and your books are mine
For I loved the girl who read them for her virtue
And now you have my vices and my name.

OTHER TIMES

Midsummer's liquid evenings linger even
And melt the wind in autumn, when bonfires
Burn books and bones, and lend us foreign faces.
At such a heart's November I might wish
There was some way back through the calendar
Again to find you and to lose your love.

I might—but there's no eager winter weather
To my remembering. Our appetites
Were satisfied with spring, and cloyed by June.
If August brought us famine... Well, no matter.
It serves us right that when I'd think of you
My memory comes hankering back to autumn.

The gloam rains slowly; fireworks kick with green,
Attach all marigoldal to the hand.
A weasel dancing by the sallows calls
Windsor to mind, and when you went tip-toe
By the breathing statue of the Copper Horse
For bashful fear it would come down to us.

The roundabouts and swings wear canvas shrouds
In gardens our ghosts visit. A bat walks—
Hare-lip, shrill membrane, hooks—as it were you.
A bat's newfangled walk, as it were you.
Dear flackering bat, or ghost, my faithless head
Has not forgot you, though our haunts are gone.

And you have gone, though your autumnity
Remains to vex me in each hip and haw
Which early frosts have ripened to perfection.
'Do not remember me for I am here
At other times,' you said. At other times
I can remember but have loved enough.

A MOTH

'See, there, her face behind us, on the pane
That runs with night. She watches jealously
While I undress your shadow on the ceiling.
She comes and goes between us if we nap
Too near the grate, or walk before this lamp,
Sleep-walkers leading the blind colts of sleep
For them to fill the steps we make for them.'

'Put out the light. There is no one behind us—
Only a moth who wants to die too soon.
Or let her in, and welcome, for she'll find
Fire's not so hot nor flame so flattering when
You have no choice but burning, and that's hard.
Now, sleep, and no more dreams. I'll leave my best
Shoes, heels under, to ride away nightmare.'

A SONG OF SIXPENCE

My thumbs prick upon consequence.
Moths brush the wafers of grass
And the stickleback feels his thimble
Underwater house tremble
Where their warfare was.
In the black stream is sixpence.

Into my purse I put sixpence,
Nor bite my little finger at the words
Ants whisper round the chambers
Of a tussock of those strangers
Unwelcome to our tryst in the dark woods.
My thumbs prick upon consequence.

To pay whoever comes with no pretence
I have picked up this silver sixpence.
My thumbs prick upon consequence.

LISTENERS

Listening silence in the glass
The listening rain against.
All in the silent house asleep,
The rain and the glass awake;
All night they listen for a noise
No one is there to make.

All in the silent house asleep,
The rain and the glass awake;
Listening silence in the glass
The listening rain against.
All night they listen for a noise
Their silence cannot break.

Index of titles

About a Maypole, 12
Absence of Nettles, An, 86
Admonition on a Rainy Afternoon, 44
After Simplicius, 22
Agnus Dei, 75
All Hallows, 67
Anniversary, 89
At Chartreuse de la Verne, 7
At Last, 96
At the Circus, 25

Bat in a Box, A, 93
Birthright, 18
Bit of Honesty, A, 55

Castle of the Perfect Ones, The, 51
Catching Leaves, 52
Charm against Amnesia, A, 58
Charm against Bad Dreams, A, 14
Childhood Incident, 61
Christmas Eve, 101
Christmas Witness, The, 56
Clown, The, 10
Cockerel, The, 36
Cockle-shells at Pagglesham, 16
Crowson, 78
Cure, The, 4

Darker Ends, 94
Dedications, 104
Devil in Me, The, 9
Devil's Jig, The, 32
Dorothy Wordsworth's Sonnet, 15
Down Darkening, 39

Ember, The, 40
English Education, An, 31
Excellent Match, An, 90

Familiar Terms, 100
Finch, 34
Fishing, 77
Frogs, The, 48

Gathering Sticks, 87
Going to the Dogs, 63
Golden Knot, A, 97
Gone Out, 88
Good-Morning in a Catholic Country, 2

Hares Dancing, 43
Henry James, 74
Hospital Incident, 45

In Memoriam John Cowper Powys, 66
In More's Hotel, 68
Interview, 71

Lark, The, 98
Lark at Dayspring, The, 20
Listeners, 108
Loaf of Bread, A, 91

Margaretting, 42
Memory, 50
Moon Fever, 57

Moth, A, 106
My Companion, 8
My Uncle, 72
Night Watch, 103
Not Looking, 84

On a Leaf Used as a Book-Mark, 49
Only Way, The, 13
Opal, 6
O Polly Dear, 41
Other Times, 105

Pastourelle, 29
Prize, The, 37
Prologue to a Mask of the Seven Deadly Sins, 65

Rain in the Eaves, The, 47
Rain Upon the Roof, The, 59
Rat, The, 19
Reading Robert Southey to my Daughter, 69
Riposte, 64
Ropes, 83
Rough Old Joker, 81

Same Song, The, 92
Shadows, 99
Sisters, The, 53
Small Mercy, A, 82
Song of Sixpence, A, 107
Song Talk, 35
Spider, The, 23
Stoat, The, 102

Task, The, 26
To a Young Poet, 60
Touching Treacle, 11
Traveller in the Evening, The, 3

Travelling to my Second Marriage on the Day
    of the First Moonshot, 73
Trout, A, 85

Valediction, A, 33
Vigils, 21
Violin, 2

Walking in Cloud, 17
Well-Spring, The, 28
Wideawake Water, 95
Winter More, 30
Without Prejudice, 54
Words on the Wind, 1

Index of first lines

Above all other nights that night be blessed, 64
A leaf, blown back towards the pool, 49
As a boy I dreamt of a place called Margaretting, 42
As I walked home a stoat ran round, 102
At Chartreuse de la Verne the very bees, 7
At Dormans Land I saw a skein of girls, 12
At thirteen he went fishing for stars, 77

Bees (some believe) on Christmas Eve, 21
Before I went to school my grandmother, 31
Begrudged by the promising pencraft of my name, 104

Come Friday night my father's public vice, 63

Darklong I walked in the long dark, 37
Dear, if one day you hear my heart, 96
Do not suppose your tender touch, 44
Down darkening or darkening down, 39
Down in the wood the boys walk wild, 82

Even on good days I can feel him there, 8

Few know as well as I do, 23

Happens this spring won't freeze, and that is something, 28
Have you forgotten sitting on the stairs, 40
He can cut straight down oak, to shape it well, 81
He died at the proper time, on Christmas Day, 78
Henry James, top hat in hand, important, boring, 74
Here's my hand turned to shadows on the wall, 104

I am said to be made in the image of a mystery, 65
I am your glass, and mirror everywhere, 90
I call midwinter back to hear you cry, 56
I heard a voice calling, 1
I like nettles, but I took, 86
In a muck sweat you quarrel with them all, 60
In the small hours of the needful night, 97
I saw a dead rat on the road, 19
I saw a man nailed to a tree, 10
I saw two frogs under a stone, 48
I went to the road for food, and found, 91

Knowing the horror of the house, 66

Listening silence in the glass, 108
Listen. It is the rain upon the roof, 59
LORD GEORGE SANGER'S CIRCUS (*For One Night*, 25
Love is the name they give out in Tasmania, 55

Midsummer's liquid evenings linger even, 105
Mr Robert Southey had the makings of a haberdasher, 69
My mother's mother was a witch, 18
My thumbs prick upon consequence, 107
My uncle's hands were the colour of tobacco, 72

No name you know reminds you now, 58

Oh how I wish that I was there, 41
Once as a child I saw the willows, 67
Once, once I stood, 43
On Christmas Eve in ivory air, 101
One summer day at noon in our family kitchen, 61
On the shore, 75

Quick snow is falling, melting as it falls, 53

Seek not to be her shadow for, 99
'See, there, her face behind us, on the pane, 106

Sheets washed in rain-water, 14
She tells me when she was a girl and used to point her toe, 13
Snow in the wind and pine-smoke blown back, 87
Some say the nightingale improves his song, 35

'Thanks be to God,' most of the neighbours say, 2
The boy lies dying in the hospital, 45
The boy you were caught leaves that fell, 52
The cockerel wakes his neighbours up, 36
The devil in me coming to a head, 9
The devil's asleep in the place of the dead, 32
The eaves drip rain. It is the eaves, 47
The finch, an inch or two of fire, 34
The Lady Memory disguised in moonlight, 50
The lark from his nest in a hoofprint springs, 98
The long cold cracked and I walked in the cracks, 93
There is no more to be said, 33
The smell of cockle-shells at Pagglesham, 16
The thing about the opal is, 6
The traveller hasteth in the evening, 3
This is the scene to which I keep returning, 57
This is the wooden wedding, 89
Time is a dream and all we do, 22
Too bad for the wood, 2
To Spindle, Shears, and Rod, 54
Treacle, when touched, will always disappoint, 11

Up I got and walking early, 20

Waiting for you, I sat and watched a trout, 85
Walking in cloud a man becomes, 17
Washing sleep away in a bowl of warm rain, 95
Wasn't it just that, 75
Watching for my son to fall asleep, I fell asleep first, 103
Watching the old man and the young man, 83

We got into the carriage. It was hot, 73
What's it like, though, being you? 71

Whenever you leave the house I write a poem, 88
'When he was born he cried too much, 4
When it was Winter what I saw, 30
When I was a boy I was set a certain task, 26
William was on his way to say good-bye, 15
You dream a song and I begin to sing it, 92
You hear her voice in the long grass, 29
You'll eat no honey in that bee-hive house, 51
You notice I never look at you when I speak? 84
You say I love you for your lies? 100

GREENWICH EXCHANGE BOOKS

All books are paperbacks unless otherwise stated

POETRY

Adam's Thoughts in Winter *by Warren Hope*
Warren Hope's poems have appeared from time to time in a number of literary periodicals, pamphlets and anthologies on both sides of the Atlantic. They appeal to lovers of poetry everywhere. His poems are brief, clear, frequently lyrical, characterised by wit, but often distinguished by tenderness. The poems gathered in this first book-length collection counter the brutalising ethos of contemporary life, speaking of and for the virtues of modesty, honesty and gentleness in an individual, memorable way.
2000 • 47 pages • ISBN 1-871551-40-4

Baudelaire: Les Fleurs du Mal *Translated by F.W. Leakey*
Selected poems from *Les Fleurs du Mal* are translated with parallel French texts and are designed to be read with pleasure by readers who have no French as well as those who are practised in the French language.
F.W. Leakey was Professor of French in the University of London. As a scholar, critic and teacher he specialised in the work of Baudelaire for 50 years and published a number of books on the poet.
2001 • 153 pages • ISBN 1-871551-10-2

'The Last Blackbird' and other poems by Ralph Hodgson *edited and introduced by John Harding*
Ralph Hodgson (1871-1962) was a poet and illustrator whose most influential and enduring work appeared to great acclaim just prior to and during the First World War. His work is imbued with a spiritual passion for the beauty of creation and the mystery of existence. This new selection brings together, for the first time in 40 years, some of the most beautiful and powerful 'hymns to life' in the English language.
John Harding lives in London. He is a freelance writer and teacher and is Ralph Hodgson's biographer.
2004 • 70 pages • ISBN 1-871551-81-1

Lines from the Stone Age *by Sean Haldane*
Reviewing Sean Haldane's 1992 volume *Desire in Belfast*, Robert Nye wrote in *The Times* that "Haldane can be sure of his place among the English poets." This place is not yet a conspicuous one, mainly because his early volumes appeared in Canada and because he has earned his living by other

means than literature. Despite this, his poems have always had their circle of readers. The 60 previously unpublished poems of *Lines from the Stone Age* – "lines of longing, terror, pride, lust and pain" – may widen this circle.
2000 • 53 pages • ISBN 1-871551-39-0

Shakespeare's Sonnets *by Martin Seymour-Smith*
Martin Seymour-Smith's outstanding achievement lies in the field of literary biography and criticism. In 1963 he produced his comprehensive edition, in the old spelling, of *Shakespeare's Sonnets* (here revised and corrected by himself and Peter Davies in 1998). With its landmark introduction and its brilliant critical commentary on each sonnet, it was praised by William Empson and John Dover Wilson. Stephen Spender said of him "I greatly admire Martin Seymour-Smith for the independence of his views and the great interest of his mind"; and both Robert Graves and Anthony Burgess described him as the leading critic of his time. His exegesis of the *Sonnets* remains unsurpassed.
2001 • 194 pages • ISBN 1-871551-38-2

Wilderness *by Martin Seymour-Smith*
This is Martin Seymour-Smith's first publication of his poetry for more than twenty years. This collection of 36 poems is a fearless account of an inner life of love, frustration, guilt, laughter and the celebration of others. He is best known to the general public as the author of the controversial and bestselling *Hardy* (1994).
1994 • 52 pages • ISBN 1-871551-08-0

LITERATURE & BIOGRAPHY

Matthew Arnold and 'Thyrsis' *by Patrick Carill Connolly*
Matthew Arnold (1822-1888) was a leading poet, intellect and aesthete of the Victorian epoch. He is now best known for his strictures as a literary and cultural critic, and educationist. After a long period of neglect, his views have come in for a re-evaluation. Arnold's poetry remains less well known, yet his poems and his understanding of poetry, which defied the conventions of his time, were central to his achievement.
The author traces Arnold's intellectual and poetic development, showing how his poetry gathers its meanings from a lifetime's study of European literature and philosophy. Connolly's unique exegesis of 'Thyrsis' draws upon a wide-ranging analysis of the pastoral and its associated myths in both classical and native cultures. This study shows lucidly and in detail how Arnold encouraged the intense reflection of the mind on the subject placed before it, believing in " ... the all importance of the choice of the

subject, the necessity of accurate observation; and subordinate character of expression."

Patrick Carill Connolly gained his English degree at Reading University and taught English literature abroad for a number of years before returning to Britain. He is now a civil servant living in London.

2004 • 180 pages • ISBN 1-871551-01-61-7

The Author, the Book and the Reader by *Robert Giddings*
This collection of essays analyses the effects of changing technology and the attendant commercial pressures on literary styles and subject matter. Authors covered include Charles Dickens, Tobias George Smollett, Mark Twain, Dr Johnson and John le Carré.

1991 • 220 pages • illustrated • ISBN 1-871551-01-3

Aleister Crowley and the Cult of Pan by *Paul Newman*
Few more nightmarish figures stalk English literature than Aleister Crowley (1875-1947), poet, magician, mountaineer and agent provocateur. In this groundbreaking study, Paul Newman dives into the occult mire of Crowley's works and fishes out gems and grotesqueries that are by turns ethereal, sublime, pornographic and horrifying. Like Oscar Wilde before him, Crowley stood in "symbolic relationship to his age" and to contemporaries like Rupert Brooke, G.K. Chesterton and the Portuguese modernist, Fernando Pessoa. An influential exponent of the cult of the Great God Pan, his essentially 'pagan' outlook was shared by major European writers as well as English novelists like E.M. Forster, D.H. Lawrence and Arthur Machen.

Paul Newman lives in Cornwall. Editor of the literary magazine *Abraxas*, he has written over ten books.

2004 • 223 pages • ISBN 1-871551-66-8

John Dryden by *Anthony Fowles*
Of all the poets of the Augustan age, John Dryden was the most worldly. Anthony Fowles traces Dryden's evolution from 'wordsmith' to major poet. This critical study shows a poet of vigour and technical panache whose art was forged in the heat and battle of a turbulent polemical and pamphleteering age. Although Dryden's status as a literary critic has long been established, Fowles draws attention to Dryden's neglected achievements as a translator of poetry. He deals also with the less well-known aspects of Dryden's work – his plays and occasional pieces.

Born in London and educated at the Universities of Oxford and Southern California, Anthony Fowles began his career in filmmaking before becoming an author of film and television scripts and more than twenty books. Readers

will welcome the many contemporary references to novels and film with which Fowles illuminates the life and work of this decisively influential English poetic voice.
2003 • 292 pages • ISBN 1-871551-58-7

The Good That We Do *by John Lucas*
John Lucas' book blends fiction, biography and social history in order to tell the story of his grandfather, Horace Kelly. Headteacher of a succession of elementary schools in impoverished areas of London, 'Hod' Kelly was also a keen cricketer, a devotee of the music hall, and included among his friends the great Trade Union leader, Ernest Bevin. In telling the story of his life, Lucas has provided a fascinating range of insights into the lives of ordinary Londoners from the First World War until the outbreak of the Second World War. Threaded throughout is an account of such people's hunger for education, and of the different ways government, church and educational officialdom ministered to that hunger. *The Good That We Do* is both a study of one man and of a period when England changed, drastically and forever.
John Lucas is Professor of English at Nottingham Trent University and is a poet and critic.
2001 • 214 pages • ISBN 1-871551-54-4

In Pursuit of Lewis Carroll *by Raphael Shaberman*
Sherlock Holmes and the author uncover new evidence in their investigations into the mysterious life and writing of Lewis Carroll. They examine published works by Carroll that have been overlooked by previous commentators. A newly discovered poem, almost certainly by Carroll, is published here.
Amongst many aspects of Carroll's highly complex personality, this book explores his relationship with his parents, numerous child friends, and the formidable Mrs Liddell, mother of the immortal Alice. Raphael Shaberman was a founder member of the Lewis Carroll Society and a teacher of autistic children.
1994 • 118 pages • illustrated • ISBN 1-871551-13-7

Liar! Liar!: Jack Kerouac – Novelist *by R.J. Ellis*
The fullest study of Jack Kerouac's fiction to date. It is the first book to devote an individual chapter to every one of his novels. *On the Road, Visions of Cody* and *The Subterraneans* are reread in-depth, in a new and exciting way. *Visions of Gerard* and *Doctor Sax* are also strikingly reinterpreted, as are other daringly innovative writings, like 'The Railroad Earth' and his "try at a spontaneous *Finnegans Wake*" – *Old Angel Midnight*. Neglected

writings, such as *Tristessa* and *Big Sur*, are also analysed, alongside better-known novels such as *Dharma Bums* and *Desolation Angels*. R.J. Ellis is Senior Lecturer in English at Nottingham Trent University.

1999 • 295 pages • ISBN 1-871551-53-6

Musical Offering *by Yolanthe Leigh*
In a series of vivid sketches, anecdotes and reflections, Yolanthe Leigh tells the story of her growing up in the Poland of the 1930s and the Second World War. These are poignant episodes of a child's first encounters with both the enchantments and the cruelties of the world; and from a later time, stark memories of the brutality of the Nazi invasion, and the hardships of student life in Warsaw under the Occupation. But most of all this is a record of inward development; passages of remarkable intensity and simplicity describe the girl's response to religion, to music, and to her discovery of philosophy.
Yolanthe Leigh was formerly a Lecturer in Philosophy at Reading University.

2000 • 57 pages • ISBN: 1-871551-46-3

Norman Cameron *by Warren Hope*
Norman Cameron's poetry was admired by W.H. Auden, celebrated by Dylan Thomas and valued by Robert Graves. He was described by Martin Seymour-Smith as, "one of ... the most rewarding and pure poets of his generation ..." and is at last given a full length biography. This eminently sociable man, who had periods of darkness and despair, wrote little poetry by comparison with others of his time, but always of a consistently high quality – imaginative and profound.

2000 • 221 pages • illustrated • ISBN 1-871551-05-6

STUDENT GUIDES

Greenwich Exchange Student Guides are critical studies of major or contemporary serious writers in English and selected European languages. The series is for the student, the teacher and 'common readers' and is an ideal resource for libraries. The *Times Educational Supplement* praised these books, saying, "The style of these guides has a pressure of meaning behind it. Students should learn from that ... If art is about selection, perception and taste, then this is it."

(ISBN prefix 1-871551- applies)

The series includes:
W.H. Auden by Stephen Wade (36-6)
Honoré de Balzac by Wendy Mercer (48-X)
William Blake by Peter Davies (27-7)
The Brontës by Peter Davies (24-2)
Robert Browning by John Lucas (59-5)
Samuel Taylor Coleridge by Andrew Keanie (64-1)
Joseph Conrad by Martin Seymour-Smith (18-8)
William Cowper by Michael Thorn (25-0)
Charles Dickens by Robert Giddings (26-9)
Emily Dickinson by Marnie Pomeroy (68-4)
John Donne by Sean Haldane (23-4)
Ford Madox Ford by Anthony Fowles (63-3)
The Stagecraft of Brian Friel by David Grant (74-9)
Robert Frost by Warren Hope (70-6)
Thomas Hardy by Sean Haldane (33-1)
Seamus Heaney by Warren Hope (37-4)
Gerard Manley Hopkins by Sean Sheehan (77-3)
James Joyce by Michael Murphy (73-0)
Philip Larkin by Warren Hope (35-8)
Poets of the First World War by John Greening (79-X)
Laughter in the Dark – The Plays of Joe Orton by Arthur Burke (56-0)
Philip Roth by Paul McDonald (72-2)
Shakespeare's *Macbeth* by Matt Simpson (69-2)
Shakespeare's *Othello* by Matt Simpson (71-4)
Shakespeare's *The Tempest* by Matt Simpson (75-7)
Shakespeare's Non-Dramatic Poetry by Martin Seymour-Smith (22-6)
Shakespeare's Sonnets by Martin Seymour-Smith (38-2)
Tobias Smollett by Robert Giddings (21-8)
Dylan Thomas by Peter Davies (78-1)
Alfred, Lord Tennyson by Michael Thorn (20-X)
William Wordsworth by Andrew Keanie (57-9)